Mouth

Julie Murray

Peachtree

Abdo
YOUR BODY
Kids

abdopublishing.com

Published by Abdo Kids, a division of ABDO, PO Box 398166, Minneapolis, Minnesota 55439.
Copyright © 2016 by Abdo Consulting Group, Inc. International copyrights reserved in all countries.
No part of this book may be reproduced in any form without written permission from the publisher.

Printed in the United States of America, North Mankato, Minnesota.

102015

012016

THIS BOOK CONTAINS
RECYCLED MATERIALS

Photo Credits: iStock, Shutterstock

Production Contributors: Teddy Borth, Jennie Forsberg, Grace Hansen

Design Contributors: Candice Keimig, Dorothy Toth

Library of Congress Control Number: 2015941973

Cataloging-in-Publication Data

Murray, Julie.
 Mouth / Julie Murray.
   p. cm. -- (Your body)
ISBN 978-1-68080-160-6 (lib. bdg.)
Includes index.
1. Mouth--Juvenile literature.   I. Title.
612.3/1--dc23
                    2015941973

Table of Contents

Mouth

The mouth is part of your body. Tim and Todd touch their mouths.

5

You can move your mouth.

Jake smiles. Karen frowns.

Lips are part of your mouth.

You kiss with your lips.

9

Teeth are inside your mouth.

Jack brushes his teeth.

The tongue is part of your mouth. You use it to taste.

13

Marco eats an apple.

It tastes sweet.

You use your mouth to talk.

Mike talks to his dad.

Animals have mouths.

A hippo has a big mouth!

How **wide** can you open your mouth?

20

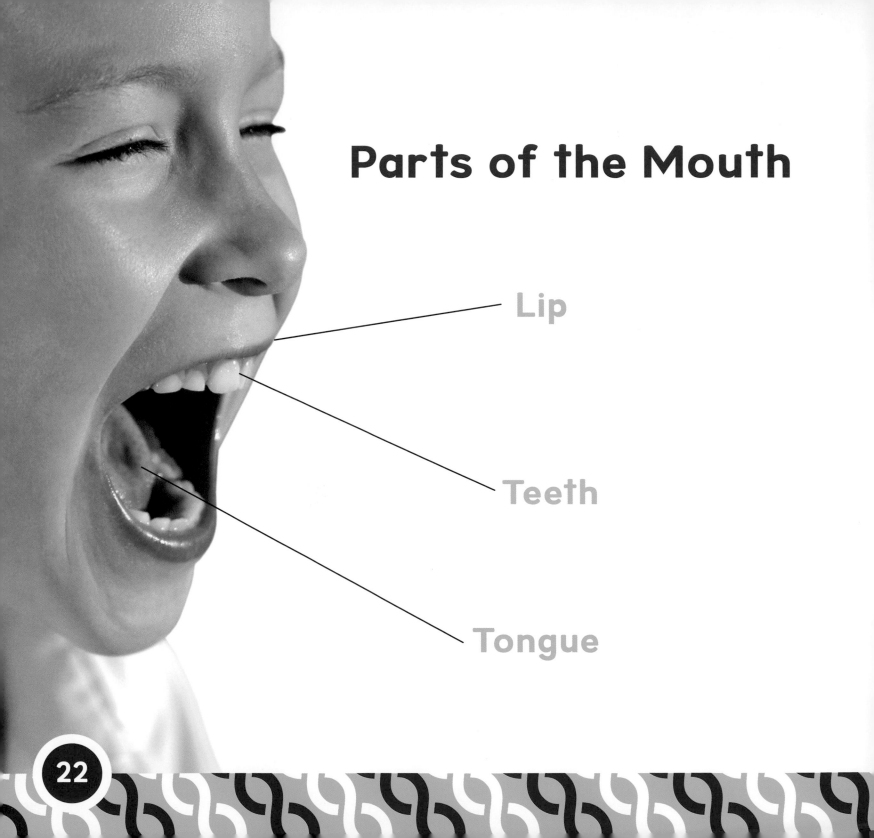

Parts of the Mouth

Lip

Teeth

Tongue

22

Glossary

frown
shows unhappiness by turning down the corners of the mouth.

wide
far from side to side.

Index

abdokids.com

Use this code to log on to abdokids.com and access crafts, games, videos, and more!

Abdo Kids Code:
YMK1606